# Diet recommendations for TCM - Bladder - Moist heat in the bladder

Please check these recommendations always with a nutrition consultant, therapist, doctor or dietician. The recipes and the list of ingredients are supporting the conventional medical therapy.
The calorie disclosures of fresh ingredients (fruit and vegetables) vary according to quality and time of harvest. The contents were checked by a dietician and a nutrition consultant for the Traditional Chinese Medicine (TCM).

Author:
©2019 Josef Miligui
www.ebns.at

Source:
The lists are created from the EBNS database for nutritional counseling. The database is used by dietitians, therapists and doctors for advising the patient / client.

Literature:
The specialist literature and the training documents of the German and Austrian dietary and traditional Chinese medicine serve as a knowledge base. We have used the documents as a basis of knowledge, adapted it to our experience and completed them.
http://di-book.com

Production and publishing:
BoD – Books on Demand, Norderstedt
ISBN: 9783746096445

**Diet recommendations for TCM - Bladder - Moist heat in the bladder**

# 1 Treatment strategy

Remove heat and moisture, open waterways. Hot NO, warm NO (only spicy YES), neutral and refreshing YES (except sour NO), cold bitter and salty YES sweet and sour NO.

# 2 Avoid

Bitter, dehydrating and all that creates moisture.

# 3 Breakfast

|  | kkal. per serving |
| --- | --- |
| Adzuki Bean and Rice Soup | 199 |
| Apple sauce with raisins | 73 |
| Barley mash with steamed pear | 113 |
| Barley porridge with cranberries | 152 |
| Barley soup | 265 |
| Bean paste piquant sweet | 311 |
| Cardamom water | 16 |
| Champignon rice | 410 |
| Corn coffee with cardamom | 3 |
| Cucumber soup | 95 |
| Fish soup with rosemary | 271 |
| Kohlrabi in chervil sauce with potatoes | 187 |
| Legumes | 31 |
| Miso soup with tofu | 51 |
| Oat Congee | 162 |
| Potato with dandelion salad | 162 |
| Rice porridge with shrubs (seeds) Yi Yi Ren | 211 |
| Rice with parsnips | 206 |
| Roasted millet with Celery sticks | 400 |
| Rosemary Potatoes | 188 |
| Tae from Dandelionroots | 1 |

# 4   Snack

# 5   Lunch

# 6  Afternoon

# 7  Dinner

# 8 Any time

# 9 Recipes

(rec.) = You can use more.
(little) = You should use less than specified
(no) omit.

## 9.1 Adzuki Bean and Rice Soup

Reduces moisture, directs down, reduces gastrointestinal heat, builds up essence, strengthens muscles after heat illness, builds up body fluids.
Cooking time approx. 2 hours
Calories p. portion: 199
1 portion

### Quantity of ingredients:

Adzuki beans 8 table spoons / 40g. (rec.) - neutral - sweet, sour.............. water
Rice round grain 2 table spoons / 20g. (rec.) - neutral - sweet................. metal
Water 1 1/2 cups / 200g. (yes) - cool - salty..............................................earth
Honey 1 table spoon / 8g. () - cold - sweet................................................earth

### Cooking instructions:

Boil soaked adzuki beans and round grain rice in a ratio of 4: 1 in water until a thin pub has formed. Sweet as needed; possibly puree.

Effect: This recipe strengthens kidney, spleen and stomach and is particularly suitable for mothers with too little milk flow.

## 9.2 Apple sauce with raisins

Nourishes fluids, reduces stomach heat, strengthens spleen, harmonizes stomach, moisturizes, relaxes, builds up Qi.
Cooking time approx. 25 min
Calories p. portion: 74
10 portions
Allergens: O

### Quantity of ingredients:

Apple (sweet) 2,2 lbs / 1000g. (yes) - cool - sweet, sour............................earth
Water 1/2 cup / 100g. (yes) - cool - salty...................................................earth
Raisins 1/8 lbs - 2oz / 50g. (yes) - warm - sweet........................................earth

### Cooking instructions:

Wash, peel and quarter the apples and remove the core. Put the apples with the water in a pot. Wash the raisins with hot water and add them.

Cook at low heat for about 10 minutes, then allow to cool. For children up to 10 months, mash in the blender finely. For the larger ones, crush with the potato steamer. Fill and seal in a freezer or empty yoghurt jug. Close the yoghurt jug. Freeze in the shock freezer.

If necessary, thaw at room temperature for about 6 hours. (Lasting about 4 months).

The fruit mousse is intended as dessert or intermediate meal. It has an anti-digestive effect. In case of diarrhea give better banana.

## 9.3   Asparagus and herb ragout

Nourishes Yin from lung kidney blood and liver, produces humors, feeds Yin, moisturizes, relaxes, builds up Qi, spreads, strengthens spleen and liver, regulates Qi flow.

Cooking time approx. 30 min
Calories p. portion: 168
4 portions
Allergens: GL

**Quantity of ingredients:**
Basic recipe for a vegetable soup (nutritious) 2 cups / 500g. (yes) - neutral - * *
Lemon peel 1/2 piece / 3g. (yes) - cool - bitter ............................................. fire
Coriander 1/4 teaspoon / 1g. (yes) - warm - acrid ................................... metal
Nutmeg 1 pinch / 0,3g. (little) - warm - acrid............................................. metal
Asparagus (green or white) 1,8 lbs / 800g. (yes) - cool - sweet, bitter ....... earth
Parsley 1 Bunch / 125g. (yes) - warm - bitter ........................................... wood
Crème fraiche cheese 2 table spoons / 30g. () - neutral - sweet ............... earth
Lemon juice 1 teaspoon / 3g. () - cold - sour............................................. wood
Potato 7/8 lbs / 400g. (yes) - neutral - sweet.............................................. earth

**Cooking instructions:**
Cook potatoes with plenty of salted water about 20 min. until soft.
Heat the vegetable stock with lemon zest, coriander and nutmeg till it boil. Cook the peeled and sliced asparagus in it.
Drain asparagus in a sieve. Collect the cooking liquid.
In the blender mix 200 g of cooked asparagus (the lower ends), cooking liquid and parsley to a smooth sauce. Beat the sauce with crème fraîche until smooth. Add asparagus and heat again and season with lemon juice, salt and pepper. Serve with the potatoes.

## 9.4 Barley mash with steamed pear

Moisturizes lungs, cools heat, reduced hot lung mucus, produces humors, moisturizes, relaxes, builds up Qi, spreads, forces spleen, diuretic, moisturizes intestines, relaxes, builds up Qi, spreads.
Cooking time approx. 25 min
Calories p. portion: 114
5 portions
Allergens: A

### Quantity of ingredients:

Water 10 cups / 1200g. (yes) - cool - salty ................................................earth
Barley 1 cup / 120g. (rec.) - cool - sweet, little salty ..................................earth
Ginger fresh 2 slices / 2g. (yes) - warm - acrid.........................................metal
Cardamom 3 capsules / 1g. (yes) - warm - acrid......................................metal
Salt 1 pinch / 1g. (yes) - cold - salty ........................................................water
Pear 1 piece / 200g. (little) - cool - sweet, sour ...........................................earth
Sugar cane sugar 1/2 teaspoon / 5g. (little) - cool - sweet .........................earth

### Cooking instructions:

Grind coarse the barley and roast it dry. Add hot water, add ginger and cardamom and let it swell to a pulp in low heat. Peel and dice the pear and boil for 10 minutes with a little water. At the end, add the stewed pear, a little butter and sweetener.
Variant: If you want to go fast, you can use barley flakes instead of shot.

## 9.5 Barley porridge with cranberries

Strengthens essence. Strengthens spleen, cools bladder, diuretic, relaxes, builds Qi, distributes. Strengthens middle, moisturizes dryness.
Cooking time approx. 2 hours
Calories p. portion: 152
4 portions
Allergens: A

### Quantity of ingredients:

Water 10 cups / 1200g. (yes) - cool - salty ................................................earth
Barley 1 cup / 120g. (rec.) - cool - sweet, little salty ..................................earth
Ginger fresh 2 slices / 2g. (yes) - warm - acrid.........................................metal
Cardamom 3 capsules / 1g. (yes) - warm - acrid......................................metal
Salt 1 pinch / 1g. (yes) - cold - salty ........................................................water
Cranberries 5/8 lbs - 8oz / 250g. (yes) - cool - sour .........................................*
Cocoa 1 pinch / 1g. () - warm - sweet, bitter................................................fire
Barley malt 1 table spoon / 15g. (yes) - cool - sweet...............................earth
Lemon Balm (fresh) 2-4 leaves / 3g. (yes) - cool - sour ...........................metal

**Cooking instructions:**
Boil the barley with water, ginger and cardamom pods in a large saucepan. Close pot with a lid and cook over low heat for about 2 hours.

For 2 servings of cooked barley porridge, place about 2 ladles in a bowl. Stir with sunflower seeds, malt, cocoa powder and a pinch of salt. Stir fresh berries into the porridge and serve sprinkled with fresh mint or lemon balm.

Tip: The precooked barley porridge (without fruit) can be kept well in the fridge and used for both sweet and savory dishes, e.g. with stewed vegetables or fruit compote.

## 9.6  Barley soup

Works neutral to slightly warming and relaxes the Qi flow. Helps with loss of appetite and diarrhea due to spleen
weakness. With weak spleen qi, one should often eat salty soups for breakfast.
Cooking time approx. 25 min
Calories p. portion: 265
2 portions
Allergens: A

**Quantity of ingredients:**
Barley 1 cup / 120g. (rec.) - cool - sweet, little salty ....................................earth
Salt 1 pinch / 1g. (yes) - cold - salty ..........................................................water
Ginger fresh 1/2 teaspoon / 1g. (yes) - warm - acrid.................................metal
Olive oil 1 table spoon / 10g. (little) - cool - sweet....................................earth
Parsley 3 table spoons / 30g. (yes) - warm - bitter.....................................wood
Water 1 1/2 cups / 240g. (yes) - cool - salty...............................................earth

**Cooking instructions:**
Roast the barley in the pan, then grind it to the ground, and boil with water, some salt and ginger to a mash. Before
serving add oil and parsley.

Variant: You can add a better taste to the dish if you cook it with prepared vegetable or meat broth.

## 9.7   Basic recipe for a chicken broth worming

Strengthens Qi and blood, is very warm.
Cooking time approx. 2-3 hours
Calories p. portion: 90
9 portions
Allergens: L

### Quantity of ingredients:
Chicken meat 1/2 piece / 600g. (yes) - warm - sweet ............................... wood
Carrot 2 pieces / 150g. (yes) - neutral - sweet ...........................................earth
Leek 1 stick / 45g. (yes) - warm - acrid ...................................................... metal
Celery root 1 piece / 500g. (yes) - cool - sweet...........................................earth
Ginger fresh 2 slices / 2g. (yes) - warm - acrid............................................ metal
Juniper berry 1 teaspoon / 3g. (yes) - warm - sweet, acrid, bitter..................fire
Bay leaf 3 pieces / 2g. (yes) - warm - acrid ................................................ metal
Water 4 cup / 900g. (yes) - cool - salty.......................................................earth

### Cooking instructions:
Remove chicken parts from fat. Place chicken pieces in a saucepan
with hot water and heat till it boils briefly, skimming any resulting foam.
Add coarsely chopped vegetables and all spices and cook over medium
heat for 2 to 3 hours. Strain the finished soup. Throw away vegetables
and bones.
Tip: If you want to use the meat as a soup insert, take out after 45
minutes and return only the bones in the soup.
Refrigerate for later use.


## 9.8   Basic recipe for a duck broth

Forces Qi, strengthens blood and fluids, nourishes Yin, forces stomach,
cools heat, strengthens spleen and liver.
Cooking time approx. 2-3 hours
Calories p. portion: 61
6 portions
Allergens: L

### Quantity of ingredients:
Duck (heart) 5/8 oz / 200g. (rec.) - cool - sweet ........................................ wood
Water 2 cup / 450g. (yes) - cool - salty.......................................................earth
Duck (slaughtered) 1/4 lbs - 4oz / 100g. (rec.) - cool - sweet, salty........... wood
Carrot 2 pieces / 100g. (yes) - neutral - sweet ...........................................earth
Celery root 1/2 piece / 600g. (yes) - cool - sweet.......................................earth

**Cooking instructions:**
Cook duck pieces with vegetables for 2-3 hours. Sift broth through a fine sieve and refrigerate for later use.

The innards can be reused: You cut them finely and leaves them for a few minutes with fresh vegetables in the broth draw. Sprinkle with parsley before serving.

## 9.9   Basic recipe for a fish broth

Strengthens kidney Qi and Yin, strengthens blood and fluids, promotes urination.
Cooking time approx. 40 min
Calories p. portion: 128
5 portions
Allergens: DLO

**Quantity of ingredients:**
Fish pieces mixed (fresh water) 3/4 lbs / 300g. (yes) - warm - sweet, saltywater
Celery root 1/4 lbs - 4oz / 120g. (yes) - cool - sweet ..................................earth
Leek 2 inches / 10g. (yes) - warm - acrid ..................................................metal
Carrot 2 pieces / 150g. (yes) - neutral - sweet ...........................................earth
White wine 1/2 cup / 125g. () - cool - sweet, bitter, acrid...........................wood
Lemon 1/2 piece / 50g. () - cold - sour......................................................wood
Bay leaf 2 leaves / 2g. (yes) - warm - acrid ..............................................metal
Peppercorns 3 pieces / 2g. () - warm - acrid ............................................metal
Olive oil 1 table spoon / 10g. (little) - cool - sweet .....................................earth
Water 2 cup / 450g. (yes) - cool - salty.......................................................earth

**Cooking instructions:**
Fry celery, chopped carrots and leeks in olive oil, add bay leaf and peppercorns, add pieces of fish and sauté briefly. Add water, add little white wine or lemon. Simmer gently for 30 minutes. Skim off the resulting foam several times. In the end, sift the ingredients through a cloth.
Refrigerate for later use.

## 9.10 Basic recipe for a reissue soup (Congee)

Warms the stomach and spleen, harmonizes the intestine, forces Qi, reduces moisture.
Cooking time approx. 2-4 hours
Calories p. portion: 140
3 portions

**Quantity of ingredients:**
Rice variety any 1 cup / 120g. (yes) - warm - sweet.................................. metal
Water 6 cups / 700g. (yes) - cool - salty ......................................................earth

**Cooking instructions:**
Cook rice and water in a ratio of about 1: 6. The amount of water determines the thickness of the mash (matter of taste).
Put the rice in a saucepan with a heavy lid. It is important to simmer the rice after a short boil on the slightest flame, otherwise it burns.
Boil the rice for 2-4 hours. The longer it cooks, the more it strengthens. If you want to eat the dish for breakfast, you can put the rice on just before bedtime.
To be on the safe side, you should first check the behavior of your pot and cooker under observation for a similar amount of time, so that nothing burns.
Refrigerate for later use.

## 9.11 Basic recipe for a vegetable soup, nutritious

Strengthens spleen and lung, regulates Qi flow, builds up Qi, dries out, passes downwardly, strengthens stomach Qi.
Cooking time approx. 2-3 hours
Calories p. portion: 48
5 portions
Allergens: L

**Quantity of ingredients:**
Olive oil 1 table spoon / 4g. (little) - cool - sweet .........................................earth
Onion white 1 piece / 60g. (yes) - warm - acrid ..........................................metal
Carrot 3 pieces / 200g. (yes) - neutral - sweet ............................................earth
Parsnip 3/8 lbs - 6oz / 150g. (yes) - cool - bitter..............................................fire
Celery root 1 cup / 100g. (yes) - cool - sweet...............................................earth
Ginger fresh 1/2 teaspoon / 2g. (yes) - warm - acrid ...............................metal
Lemon 1/2 piece / 25g. () - cold - sour...................................................... wood
Juniper berry 6 pieces / 6g. (yes) - warm - sweet, acrid, bitter .....................fire
Thyme dried 1 pinch / 1g. (rec.) - warm - bitter .........................................metal
Lovage 1 table spoon / 3g. (yes) - warm - acrid, bitter ............................metal

Lovage 1 table spoon / 3g. (yes) - warm - acrid, bitter .............................. metal
Bay leaf 2 leaves / 1g. (yes) - warm - acrid ............................................. metal
Salt 1 pinch / 1g. (yes) - cold - salty ........................................................ water
Water 3 cups / 650g. (yes) - cool - salty ..................................................... earth

## Cooking instructions:
Cut the vegetables into cubes.
Heat oil in hot pot, fry shortly onions and vegetables.
Add cold water, then add ginger, bay leaf and lemon juice.
Season with juniper, thyme and lovage. Cover for 2 - 3 hours on a low heat and simmer.
The used vegetables should be thrown away.
The basic recipe serves as a soup base and to refine vegetables, legumes or cereals.
If you want to eat vegetable soup immediately, add the desired vegetables half an hour before. Refrigerate for later use.

## 9.12 Basmati rice + Zucchini tofu dish

Converts mucus, reduces heat, builds up Qi, nourishes fluids, harmonizes spleen and stomach, forces Lungen Qi.
Cooking time approx. 20 min
Calories p. portion: 146
4 portions
Allergens: E

## Quantity of ingredients:
Soy Tofu 5/8 lbs - 8oz / 250g. (rec.) - cool - sweet .................................... earth
Olive oil 2 table spoons / 6g. (little) - cool - sweet ..................................... earth
Coriander 1/2 teaspoon / 4g. (yes) - warm - acrid ..................................... metal
Ginger fresh 1/2 teaspoon / 4g. (yes) - warm - acrid ................................ metal
Rice Basmati 1/2 cup / 60g. (yes) - neutral - sweet ................................... metal
Water 3 cups / 200g. (yes) - cool - salty ...................................................... earth
Zucchini 1 piece / 700g. (yes) - cool - sweet ............................................... earth

## Cooking instructions:
Cut tofu cubes and marinate with olive oil, tamari, crushed coriander and ginger. Leave at least 1 hour.
Cook Basmati rice with the water. You can season with onion and cardamom.
Roast zucchini and tofu in pan in the hot oil for approx. 5-7 min.
Serve rice and tofu on a plate.
Add the parsley. Can also be used as a salad for the home and on the go.

## 9.13 Bean paste piquant sweet

Strengthens spleen, stomach and kidney, strengthens middle as well as kidneys Jang, Yin and Jing.
Cooking time approx. 1 hour
Calories p. portion: 311
1 portion
Allergens: MO

**Quantity of ingredients:**
Black beans 1 cup / 120g. (yes) - neutral - sweet ...................................water
Ginger fresh 1 inch / 3g. (yes) - warm - acrid .............................................metal
Boxhorn clover seeds 1/2 teaspoon / 2g. (yes) - warm - bitter .........................*
Tomato paste 1 table spoon / 10g. () - cold - sweet-sour .......................... wood
Olive oil 2 table spoons / 20g. (little) - cool - sweet ...................................earth
Pumpkin seed oil 1 dash / 3g. (little) - warm - sweet ..................................earth
Horseradish 1 teaspoon (grated) / 2g. (yes) - neutral - sweet, little acrid .. metal
Pepper (ground) 1 pinch / 0,5g. () - warm - acrid ......................................metal
Garlic 2 cloves / 3g. () - hot - acrid .............................................................. metal
Salt 1 pinch / 1g. (yes) - cold - salty ........................................................... water
Sugar molasses 2 table spoons / 20g. (little) - cold - sweet ......................earth
Lemon peel 1/2 piece / 1g. (yes) - cool - bitter ...............................................fire
Water 1 1/2 cups / 50g. (yes) - cool - salty...................................................earth

**Cooking instructions:**
Boil beans (with spices and ginger), drain water and puree. Season with spices.

Refine with sugar beet syrup and lemon peel.

## 9.14 Beluga lentil stew with vegetables

Tonifies Qi and blood, forces kidneys and spleen, dissipates heat and moisture.
Cooking time approx. 20 min
Calories p. portion: 201
5 portions

**Quantity of ingredients:**
Lentils 1 1/2 cups / 240g. (yes) - neutral - sweet, sour ..............................water
Water 4-5 cups / 500g. (yes) - cool - salty...................................................earth
Carrot 3 pieces / 150g. (yes) - neutral - sweet ...........................................earth
Leek 1 piece / 300g. (yes) - warm - acrid ................................................... metal
Kohlrabi 1/2 piece / 200g. (yes) - neutral - acrid, sweet ............................earth
Tomato 2 pieces / 80g. () - cold - sweet-sour ............................................. wood
Onion white 1 piece / 50g. (yes) - warm - acrid.........................................metal

Bay leaf 2 leaves / 1g. (yes) - warm - acrid ................................................ metal
Fennel 1 piece / 250g. (yes) - warm - sweet, little acrid ............................ earth
Star anise 2 pieces / 1g. (yes) - hot - acrid ................................................ metal
Juniper berry 6 pieces / 2g. (yes) - warm - sweet, acrid, bitter ..................... fire
Chili (pod or ground) 1 pinch / 0,2g. () - hot - acrid .................................... metal
Olive oil 3 table spoons / 30g. (little) - cool - sweet .................................... earth
Salt 1 pinch / 1g. (yes) - cold - salty .......................................................... water
Ginger fresh 1/2 teaspoon / 2g. (yes) - warm - acrid ................................. metal
Black caraway 1 pinch / 1g. (yes) - warm - acrid, sweet ................................... *

**Cooking instructions:**
Heat oil in hot pot. Fry onions and add diced vegetables and spices,
lentils (washed well) and salt. Cover with cold
water (3 fingers wide) and cook for 20 minutes on a low heat.
Sprinkle with fresh herbs and black cumin

Goes well with rice!

## 9.15 Black-eyed beans stew

Strengthens spleen and kidney, is very nutritious, warms the stomach
and spleen, harmonizes the intestine, forces Qi, strengthens stomach
and kidney, strengthens spleen and kidney.
Cooking time approx. 20 min
Calories p. portion: 140
5 portions

**Quantity of ingredients:**
Black-eyed peas 1 cup / 100g. (yes) - neutral - sweet, acrid ..................... water
Rice variety any 1 1/2 cups / 200g. (yes) - warm - sweet ......................... metal
Water 10 cups / 1000g. (yes) - cool - salty ................................................ earth

**Cooking instructions:**
Soak the beans overnight and strain.

In a ratio of 1: 2, simmer the beans together with the rice in the Water.
Depending on how hot the flame is and how
thin the dish should be, more water must be added.

Variation: Add vegetables fried in oil, such as carrots, celery tubers,
onions or leeks.

## 9.16 Cardamom water

Warms the middle, dissolves stagnation, directs upwards. Tonifies the kidney-Yang, nourishes bones and tendons, warms kidneys and spleen, forces stomach, dissolves flatulence, contracts, controls excessive urination, helps with digestive weakness.
Cooking time approx. 20 min
Calories p. portion: 16
4 portions

### Quantity of ingredients:
Cardamom 2 table spoons / 18g. (yes) - warm - acrid .............................. metal
Water 4 cup / 1000g. (yes) - cool - salty...................................................... earth

### Cooking instructions:
Finely crush cardamom pods in a mortar. Boil with 1 liter of water and cook gently for 10 minutes over medium heat. Fill cardamom water through a sieve in glasses and serve hot.

## 9.17 Champignon rice

Strengthens spleen, builds up Qi, directs heat down, strengthens stomach Qi, cools blood heat.
Cooking time approx. 30 min
Calories p. portion: 410
2 portions
Allergens: L

### Quantity of ingredients:
Onion white 1 piece / 50g. (yes) - warm - acrid ......................................... metal
Bay leaf 2 pieces / 1g. (yes) - warm - acrid .............................................. metal
Clove 2 pieces / 1g. (yes) - warm - acrid.................................................... metal
Basic recipe for a vegetable soup (nutritious) 7/8 lbs / 350g. (yes) - neutral - **
Rice (whole grain) 5/8 oz / 200g. (yes) - warm - sweet ............................. metal
Champignon 1/8 lbs - 2oz / 60g. (yes) - cool - sweet ................................. earth
Parsley 1/2 oz / 20g. (yes) - warm - bitter.................................................. wood
Pepper (ground) 1 pinch / 0,2g. () - warm - acrid ...................................... metal

### Cooking instructions:
Plug in the cloves in the onion. Heat the vegetable stock with the onion and the bay leaves till it boils. Add the rice to the boiling liquid, reduce the temperature to the lowest level and stir with the lid closed for 20-25 minutes.
In the meantime, wash the mushrooms, clean them, slice them, sauté briefly with a little water or sauté. Wash the parsley and chop finely.

Remove the onion from the rice, add the mushrooms and the parsley, season with pepper.

## 9.18 Clear oxen tail soup with buckthorn fruit

Forces Qi, nourishes the liver blood, good for ocular fibrillation or dry eyes, muscle tension or calf cramps due to blood deficiency.
Cooking time approx. 1-2 hours
Calories p. portion: 217
6 portions
Allergens: O

### Quantity of ingredients:
Beef Oxtail pieces 1,1 lbs / 500g. (yes) - warm - sweet...............................earth
Shiitake, dried 4-5 pieces / 4g. (yes) - neutral - sweet ...............................earth
Onion white 1 piece / 60g. (yes) - warm - acrid.........................................metal
Sake 2 table spoons / 20g. (little) - warm - sweet, bitter, acrid..................metal
Ginger fresh 1/2 teaspoon / 2g. (yes) - warm - acrid.................................metal
Bocksdorn fruits (Fructus Lycii) 1 table spoon / 8g. (yes) - cool - ............. wood

### Cooking instructions:
Soak shiitake mushrooms. Blanch oxtail slices (This removes fat and impurities).
Cook in the beef broth for 1-2 hours.
Then add the spring onions, shiitake mushrooms, rice wine, buckthorn fruits and ginger and simmer gently.

## 9.19 Corn coffee with cardamom

Dries out, passes downwardly.
Cooking time approx. 5 min
Calories p. portion: 3
1 portion

### Quantity of ingredients:
Cereal coffee 1 table spoon / 15g. (little) - warm - bitter................................fire
Cardamom 2 cores / 1g. (yes) - warm - acrid............................................metal
Water 1 cup / 120g. (yes) - cool - salty.....................................................earth

### Cooking instructions:
Boil water, coffee, sugar and cardamom. Let it set for one min before drinking.

## 9.20 Cucumber soup

Cools and moisturizes, diuretic, reduces damp heat, detoxifies, relaxes, builds up Qi, spreads, distributes mucus, passes downwardly, activates Wei Qi, forces Qi.
Cooking time approx. 20 min
Calories p. portion: 96
4 portions
Allergens: M

### Quantity of ingredients:
Olive oil 2 table spoons / 35g. (little) - cool - sweet .....................................earth
Cucumber 2 pieces / 400g. (rec.) - cold - sweet..........................................earth
Water 2 cup / 500g. (yes) - cool - salty.......................................................earth
Sage 3 leaves / 3g. (yes) - cool - bitter, spicy.................................................fire
Coriander 1 pinch / 1g. (yes) - warm - acrid ............................................... metal
Cardamom 1 pinch / 1g. (yes) - warm - acrid .............................................. metal
Salt 1 pinch / 1g. (yes) - cold - salty ......................................................... water

### Cooking instructions:
Heat oil and roast short the small cucumbers. Add Mustard seeds, coriander, cardamom and salt. Add water. Simmer for 10-15 min. Puree and decorate with fresh chopped sage.

## 9.21 Fish soup with rosemary

Strengthens kidney Qi, strengthens blood and fluids, promotes urination, regulates Qi, dries out, passes downwardly, strengthens spleen and liver, regulates Qi flow, moisturizes, relaxes, builds up Qi, spreads.
Cooking time approx. 30 min
Calories p. portion: 271
4 portions
Allergens: DLO

### Quantity of ingredients:
Basic recipe for a fish soup 2 cup / 500g. (yes) - cool - * ................................ *
Rosemary 1/2 bunch / 7g. (rec.) - warm - bitter.............................................fire
Onion (spring onion) 1 piece / 20g. (yes) - warm - acrid ........................... metal
Olive oil 2 table spoons / 35g. (little) - cool - sweet ....................................earth
Fish pieces mixed 5/8 lbs - 8oz / 250g. (yes) - warm - sweet, salty .......... water

Carrot 1 piece / 120g. (yes) - neutral - sweet ...........................................earth
Parsnip 1 piece / 180g. (yes) - cool - bitter.....................................................fire
Celery root 1 slice / 20g. (yes) - cool - sweet .............................................earth
Salt 1 pinch / 1g. (yes) - cold - salty .........................................................water
Peppercorns 2 pieces / 1g. () - warm - acrid ..............................................metal
Garlic 1 clove / 3g. () - hot - acrid .............................................................metal

**Cooking instructions:**
Fry the onion and garlic in oil. Add fish broth. Add diced carrots,
parsnips and celery. Season with salt and peppercorns. Simmer the
soup on a low heat for 25 minutes.
Wash the fish, drizzle with lemon juice, divide into pieces and add to the
soup with the pink rosemary. Cook for 5 min on low heat.
Add the chives and parsley and season the soup with the salt.

# 9.22 Grapefruit juice

Nourishes fluids, passes downwardly, forms body fluid.
Cooking time approx. 5 min
Calories p. portion: 107
1 portion
Allergens:
**Quantity of ingredients:**
Grapefruit (Pomelo) 1 cup / 250g. (yes) - cool - sweet, sour.........................fire

**Cooking instructions:**
Juice fresh grapefruit or use organic juice.

# 9.23 Indian Dal soup

Reduces internal heat and moisture, softens, passes downwardly,
strengthens spleen and liver, regulates Qi flow, moisturizes, relaxes,
builds up Qi, spreads, forces liver and kidney, reduces damp heat.
Cooking time approx. 30 min
Calories p. portion: 256
2 portions
Allergens: EN

**Quantity of ingredients:**

Lentils 3/8 lbs - 6oz / 175g. (yes) - neutral - sweet, sour ........................... water
Sesame oil 3 table spoons / 30g. (little) - cool - sweet ............................... earth
Carrot 1 piece / 100g. (yes) - neutral - sweet ........................................... earth
Onion (shallot) 1 piece / 15g. (yes) - warm - acrid, sweet ........................ metal
Water 1 1/2 cups / 200g. (yes) - cool - salty .............................................. earth
Ginger fresh 2 slices / 1g. (yes) - warm - acrid ........................................ metal
Salt 1 pinch / 0,5g. (yes) - cold - salty ..................................................... water
Soy sauce 1 teaspoon / 3g. (yes) - cold - salty .......................................... water
Parsley 1 teaspoon (chopped) / 3g. (yes) - warm - bitter ......................... wood
Thyme 1 teaspoon / 3g. (rec.) - warm - bitter .................................................. *
Basil 1 table spoon / 5g. (yes) - warm - acrid, bitter ..................................... fire

**Cooking instructions:**

Soak the lentils overnight.
in a hot pot, carrot, onion and a little ginger fry, pour water. Add the
lentils and cook until soft. Add salt or soy sauce and cook for another 10
minutes.
Stir in parsley before serving; Sprinkle thyme or basil over it.
Variant: Other herbs such as sage, rosemary or lovage allow a variety
of flavors.

## 9.24 Kohlrabi in chervil sauce with potatoes

Forces Qi, forces spleen, relieves inflammation, relaxes, spreads,
moves Qi and blood, diuretic, strengthens spleen and liver, regulates Qi
flow, cools heat, reduces internal wind and moisture, dissolves
stagnation, directs upwards.
Cooking time approx. 1 hour
Calories p. portion: 188
4 portions
Allergens: GL

**Quantity of ingredients:**

Potato 6 pieces / 450g. (yes) - neutral - sweet ........................................... earth
Basic recipe for a vegetable soup (nutritious) 1 cup / 300g. (yes) - neutral - *. *
Potato 1/4 lbs - 4oz / 100g. (yes) - neutral - sweet .................................... earth
Nutmeg 1 pinch / 0,2g. (little) - warm - acrid ............................................. metal
Lemon peel 1/2 teaspoon / 2g. (yes) - cool - bitter ...................................... fire
Ginger fresh 1/2 teaspoon / 2g. (yes) - warm - acrid ................................ metal
Lovage 1/2 teaspoon / 2g. (yes) - warm - acrid, bitter ............................... metal
Kohlrabi 3/4 lbs / 300g. (yes) - neutral - acrid, sweet ................................ earth
Salt 1 pinch / 1g. (yes) - cold - salty ........................................................ water

Pepper (ground) 1 pinch / 0,2g. () - warm - acrid ...................................... metal
Sour cream 15% fat 3 table spoons / 30g. () - cool - sour ......................... wood
Chervil dried 1 Bunch / 80g. () - warm - sweet ................................................ *

## Cooking instructions:
Boil the potatoes in salted water.
Bring half of the vegetable stock to boil. Add the diced potatoes, nutmeg, lemon zest, ginger and lovage. Cover the potatoes and cook for about 10 minutes until soft and puree them with a blender until they are smooth.
Bring remaining vegetable stock to boil. Cut kohlrabi into cubes and add, cover and cook for about 8 minutes. Stir in the potato sauce and heat everything briefly.
Puree with the mixing stick chervil and sour cream. Mix the chervil cream with the kohlrabi vegetables.
Serve with the cooked, peeled potatoes.

# 9.25 Legumes

Strengthens spleen and liver, regulates Qi flow, moisturizes, relaxes, builds up Qi, spreads, nourishes blood and Qi, diuretic, harmonizes Qi (in the middle and lower heater), detoxifies, reduces internal heat and moisture.
Cooking time approx. 30 min
Calories p. portion: 31
5 portions

## Quantity of ingredients:
Pinto beans speckled 1/4 lbs - 4oz / 100g. (yes) - neutral - sweet ............ water
Lentils 1/8 lbs - 2oz / 50g. (yes) - neutral - sweet, sour ............................. water
Peas, green 1/8 lbs - 2oz / 50g. (yes) - neutral - sweet ............................. water
Water 4 cup / 1000g. (yes) - cool - salty .................................................... earth
Lemon 1 slice / 2g. () - cold - sour ............................................................ wood
Juniper berry 6 pieces / 2g. (yes) - warm - sweet, acrid, bitter ..................... fire
Thyme 1 Twig / 3g. (rec.) - warm - bitter .......................................................... *
Rosemary 1 Twig / 3g. (rec.) - warm - bitter ................................................. fire
Carrot 1 piece / 100g. (yes) - neutral - sweet ............................................ earth
Savory 1-2 teaspoons / 5g. (yes) - warm - bitter ....................................... water
Ginger fresh a great piece / 3g. (yes) - warm - acrid ................................. metal
Bay leaf 2-3 leaves / 1g. (yes) - warm - acrid ............................................ metal
Wakame 1-2 strips / 1g. (yes) - cold - salty .............................................. water

**Cooking instructions:**
Legumes such as beans, lentils, peas or chickpeas are soaked in plenty of cold water for several hours to three days. The water should be changed every 8 hours. Then pour off soaking water and wash legumes thoroughly.

Preparation:
Cook the legumes with fresh cold water and a slice of ginger and bring to froth. Cook without lid for about 5 minutes, scooping off the foam. Only then add the following ingredients: a slice of lemon or lemon juice, crush juniper berries, thyme; (possibly 1 knife tip of asafoetida in case of severe indigestion). Add savory, sage, juniper, fenugreek seeds, carrots, bay leaves, fresh ginger, wakame algae.

Simmer on the slightest flame until beans or lentils have the desired consistency.
This base can be stored for 3-4 days in the refrigerator.

## 9.26 Miso soup with tofu

Nourish the humors, preserves the fluids, contracts, nourishes fluids, lets Qi ascend, harmonizes spleen and stomach, moisturizes, relaxes, builds up Qi, spreads, regulates Qi, warms spleen and kidney, dissolves stagnation, directs upwards.
Cooking time approx. 5 min
Calories p. portion: 51
3 portions
Allergens: E

**Quantity of ingredients:**
Wakame 1 piece / 5g. (yes) - cold - salty ................................................... water
Miso 3-4 table spoons / 30g. (yes) - neutral - salty..................................... water
Soy Tofu 1/8 lbs - 2oz / 50g. (rec.) - cool - sweet........................................ earth
Water 2 cup / 500g. (yes) - cool - salty........................................................ earth
Soy sauce 1 dash / 3g. (yes) - cold - salty.................................................... water
Onion (spring onion) 1/2 teaspoon / 6g. (yes) - warm - acrid .................... metal

**Cooking instructions:**
Boil soybean seedlings, wakame algae and diced tofu for 5 minutes. Put the miso paste in the soup plate and slowly pour over the soup. Season with Tamari sauce. Sprinkle with cutted spring onion.

## 9.27 Mung bean stew

Dissipates excess heat, is very nutritious, reduces heat and poison, softens, passes downwardly, warms the stomach and spleen, harmonizes the intestine, forces Qi, reduces moisture.
Cooking time approx. 2 hours
Calories p. portion: 665
2 portions

**Quantity of ingredients:**
Mung bean 5/8 lbs - 8oz - 500g / 300g. (rec.) - cool - sweet, salty ............ water
Sunflower oil 3 table spoons / 30g. (little) - cool - sweet ............................. earth
Amaranth 1/2 teaspoon / 2g. (rec.) - neutral - bitter, sweet ........................... fire
Cumin (Caraway seed) 1/2 teaspoon / 2g. (yes) - warm - acrid ................ metal
Coriander 1/2 teaspoon / 2g. (yes) - warm - acrid ..................................... metal
Rice round grain 1/2 cup / 60g. (rec.) - neutral - sweet ............................. metal
Water 3 cups / 300g. (yes) - cool - salty ...................................................... earth
Ginger fresh 1 inch / 3g. (yes) - warm - acrid ............................................. metal
Kombu seaweed (Saccharina japonica) 1 inch / 2g. (yes) - cold - salty .... water
Salt 1 pinch / 0,5g. (yes) - cold - salty ....................................................... water
Parsley 1 table spoon / 3g. (yes) - warm - bitter ......................................... wood

**Cooking instructions:**
Soak mung beans overnight.
Heat sunflower oil in a hot pot. Stir in the amaranth, fennel seeds, cumin and coriander and fry briefly.
admit basmati rice, some ginger and mung beans and roast briefly.
Pour water and heat till it boils.
Add a piece of kombu alga and salt.
Simmer for 1-1/2 hours.
Garnish with parsley or coriander.

## 9.28 Nettle-chard soup

Drains moisture down, strengthens blood, cools liver heat.
Cooking time approx. 30 min
Calories p. portion: 52
4 portions

**Quantity of ingredients:**

Nettles 1 handful / 10g. (yes) - neutral - bitter ........................................... wood
Chard 1 lbs / 500g. (yes) - cool - bitter, sweet.............................................earth
Salt 1 pinch / 1g. (yes) - cold - salty ........................................................ water
Water 2 cup / 400g. (yes) - cool - salty......................................................earth
Olive oil 1 table spoon / 10g. (little) - cool - sweet ....................................earth
Pepper (ground) 1 pinch / 0,5g. () - warm - acrid ...................................... metal

**Cooking instructions:**

Heat the oil in a saucepan, add the washed and finely chopped Swiss chard. Salt and let simmer for 10 minutes. Add the chopped nettles and cook for another 10 minutes. Add pepper and puree.

## 9.29 Oat Congee

Forces Qi, forces liver and spleen, moisturizes intestines, eliminates mucus, holds back sweat.
Cooking time approx. 2-4 hours
Calories p. portion: 162
3 portions
Allergens: A

**Quantity of ingredients:**

Oat 1 cup / 125g. (yes) - warm - sweet ....................................................... metal
Water 6 cups / 700g. (yes) - cool - salty......................................................earth

**Cooking instructions:**

Cook oats and water in a ratio of about 1: 6. The amount of water determines the thickness of the mash (pure matter of taste). The oats swell, so do not take much. Put the oats in a saucepan with good insulation and a heavy lid. It is important to simmer the oats after a short boil on the slightest flame, otherwise it burns. Cook the oat for 2-4 hours. The longer it cooks, the more he strengthens.

## 9.30 Potato with dandelion salad

Forces Qi, forces spleen, relieves inflammation, moisturizes, relaxes, builds up Qi, cools liver fire, reduces internal heat, softens knots, dissolves stagnation, passes downwardly, nourishes fluids und Jing, builds up Qi, spreads.
Cooking time approx. 25 min
Calories p. portion: 162
2 portions

**Quantity of ingredients:**
Potato 5/8 lbs - 8oz / 250g. (yes) - neutral - sweet.....................................earth
Onion white 1/2 piece / 20g. (yes) - warm - acrid.....................................metal
Sunflower oil 1 table spoon / 10g. (little) - cool - sweet.............................earth
Dandelion (young plants) 1/4 lbs - 4oz / 125g. (rec.) - cool - sweet, bitter ....fire
Salt 1 pinch / 1g. (yes) - cold - salty.........................................................water
Pepper white (ground) 1 pinch / 0,5g. (little) - warm - acrid.......................metal

**Cooking instructions:**
Cook the potatoes in salted water and cut into thin slices. Finely chop the onion. Now season the potatoes with oil, salt and pepper and add the dandelion and mix.

## 9.31 Pumpkin soup

Forces lungs and spleen, diuretic, forces Qi, protects liver, forces Qi, forces spleen, relieves inflammation, moisturizes, relaxes, builds up Qi, spreads, strengthens spleen and liver, regulates Qi flow, moisturizes, relaxes, builds up Qi, spreads.
Cooking time approx. 1 hour
Calories p. portion: 105
3 portions

**Quantity of ingredients:**
Pumpkin 3/4 lbs / 300g. (little) - warm - sweet............................................earth
Carrot 2 pieces / 100g. (yes) - neutral - sweet ............................................earth
Potato 2 pieces / 120g. (yes) - neutral - sweet............................................earth
Olive oil 1 table spoon / 10g. (little) - cool - sweet......................................earth
Onion white 1 piece / 50g. (yes) - warm - acrid...........................................metal
Water 1 cup / 120g. (yes) - cool - salty.......................................................earth
Parsley 1 table spoon / 7g. (yes) - warm - bitter...........................................wood
Anise (Common Fennel) 1 pinch / 1g. (yes) - warm - acrid.........................earth
Salt 1 pinch / 1g. (yes) - cold - salty.........................................................water

**Cooking instructions:**
Add the olive oil to the pan, add the diced pumpkin, diced carrots and potatoes. Roast them shortly, add the finely chopped onion, fill with water, add enough water to cover the vegetables at least 3 finger-widths. Boil at low heat.

Season with sea salt, add small cutted parsley, a pinch of anise (little). Allow to simmer for about 35 minutes. Then purée the soup and add some water, depending on the consistency of the soup.

## 9.32 Quick zucchini soup

Reduces mucus, preserves the fluids, cools liver fire, forces stomach Qi.
Cooking time approx. 10 min
Calories p. portion: 42
4 portions

### Quantity of ingredients:
Zucchini 2-3 pieces / 500g. (yes) - cool - sweet ........................................earth
Onion white 1 piece / 50g. (yes) - warm - acrid........................................ metal
Corn germ oil 2 table spoons / 6g. (yes) - neutral - sweet..........................earth
Parsley 1 table spoon / 7g. (yes) - warm - bitter...................................... wood
Chives 1 teaspoon / 3g. (yes) - warm - acrid............................................ metal
Water 2 cup / 400g. (yes) - cool - salty......................................................earth

### Cooking instructions:
Fry chopped onion in oil. Add sliced zucchini and sauté well. Pour with water. Chop parsley and chives, add and puree everything.


## 9.33 Rice porridge with shrubs (seeds) Yi Yi Ren

Warms stomach, harmonizes the intestine, forces Qi, reduces moisture, forces spleen, nourishes and forces Lunge, reduces internal heat, moves Qi and blood, diuretic, cools in internal heat.
Cooking time approx. 25 min
Calories p. portion: 212
2 portions

### Quantity of ingredients:
Water 4 cups / 450g. (yes) - cool - salty......................................................earth
Rice variety any 1 cup / 120g. (yes) - warm - sweet.................................. metal
Lemon peel 1/4 piece / 2g. (yes) - cool - bitter ...............................................fire
Coix (seeds) YiYi Ren 1/2 cup / 50g. (rec.) - cool - sweet, neutral .................. *
Cress 1 table spoon / 6g. (yes) - cool - sweet .......................................... metal

### Cooking instructions:
Cook rice porridge according to basic recipe with a half cup of Yi Yi Ren and lemon peel. Simmer for 1 hour and then sprinkle cress over it.

## 9.34 Rice with parsnips

Regulates Qi, dries out, passes downwardly, warms the stomach and spleen, harmonizes the intestine, reduces moisture. moisturizes, relaxes, spreads. distributes mucus, activates Wei Qi, forces Qi.
Cooking time approx. 45 min
Calories p. portion: 206
3 portions

### Quantity of ingredients:
Rice variety any 1 cup / 120g. (yes) - warm - sweet................................. metal
Water 1 1/2 cups / 200g. (yes) - cool - salty ................................................earth
Salt 1 pinch / 1g. (yes) - cold - salty ........................................................ water
Parsnip 3-4 pieces / 450g. (yes) - cool - bitter..............................................fire
Olive oil 1 table spoon / 10g. (little) - cool - sweet .....................................earth
Sage 1 teaspoon / 3g. (yes) - cool - bitter, spicy .............................................fire

### Cooking instructions:
Peel the parsnips and cut into slices. Fry for a short time in oil. Add the rice and fry again for a short time. Add the water and cook it at least 30 min. Sprinkle with fresh chopped sage.

## 9.35 Rice with stewed vegetables

Dissipates heat and moisture.
Cooking time approx. 20 min
Calories p. portion: 166
2 portions
Allergens: L

### Quantity of ingredients:
Rice variety any 1/2 cup / 60g. (yes) - warm - sweet................................. metal
Water 3 cups / 300g. (yes) - cool - salty ......................................................earth
Lemon peel 1 piece / 3g. (yes) - cool - bitter ...................................................fire
Water 1/2 cup / 0g. (yes) - cool - salty........................................................earth
Carrot 2 pieces / 180g. (yes) - neutral - sweet ............................................earth
Celery sticks 1/2 piece / 5g. (rec.) - cool - sweet.........................................earth
Champignon 1/2 cup / 50g. (yes) - cool - sweet............................................earth
Cress 2 table spoons / 20g. (yes) - cool - sweet ....................................... metal
Linseed oil 1 dash / 3g. (little) - neutral - sweet ..........................................earth

### Cooking instructions:
Cook rice according to basic recipe with a piece of lemon peel.
Steam chopped carrots, celery and mushrooms until soft.
Then sprinkle with cress. Then add a dash of high quality cold oil.

## 9.36 Roasted millet with Celery sticks

Strengthens spleen and kidney, diuretic, brings the liver Qi in motion, cools heat, moisturizes, relaxes, builds up Qi, spreads.
Cooking time approx. 30 min
Calories p. portion: 400
2 portions
Allergens: L

### Quantity of ingredients:
Millet 1 cup / 120g. (yes) - cool - sweet, salty.............................................earth
Water 1 1/2 cups / 240g. (yes) - cool - salty................................................earth
Celery sticks 2 rods / 50g. (rec.) - cool - sweet ..........................................earth
Water 2 table spoons / 30g. (yes) - cool - salty ...........................................earth
Salt 1 pinch / 1g. (yes) - cold - salty ........................................................water
Sage 3-4 leaves / 2g. (yes) - cool - bitter, spicy ...............................................fire
Cress 1 teaspoon / 3g. (yes) - cool - sweet...............................................metal

### Cooking instructions:
Roast millet briefly, pour over water, heat till it boils and let stand for 20 min. to swell.
Cut celery into small pieces and mix with water, salt and fresh herbs and cook for 10 min. Add to the millet. Sprinkle fresh sage or watercress over it.

## 9.37 Rosemary Potatoes

Forces Qi, forces spleen, relieves inflammation, relaxes, builds up Qi, spreads.
Cooking time approx. 30 min
Calories p. portion: 188
2 portions

### Quantity of ingredients:
Potato 6-8 pieces / 420g. (yes) - neutral - sweet.......................................earth
Olive oil 1 table spoon / 10g. (little) - cool - sweet.....................................earth
Rosemary 1 teaspoon / 2g. (rec.) - warm - bitter..........................................fire

### Cooking instructions:
Cut the potatoes into half´s, apply a little olive oil on the cut surface, then salt, sprinkle 2 - 3 rosemary needles on the potatoes.
Place the potatoes on the baking tray and bake them in the preheated oven for approx. 25 minutes to 190°C/374°F.

## 9.38 Smoothie celery carrot

Nourishes juices, strengthens spleen and liver, regulates qi flow, relaxes, builds up qi. Moves liver-qi, reduces cold-evil.
Cooking time approx. 10 Min.
Calories p. portion: 111
2 portions
Allergens: L

**Quantity of ingredients:**
Carrot 5/8 oz / 200g. (yes) - neutral - sweet ..............................................earth
Celery sticks 10 cups / 100g. (rec.) - cool - sweet.....................................earth
Apple (sweet) 5/8 oz / 200g. (yes) - cool - sweet, sour .............................earth
Basil (fresh) 2 table spoons / 5g. (yes) - warm - acrid, bitter ....................metal
Ginger fresh 1/8 oz / 5g. (yes) - warm - acrid ............................................metal
Reishi mushroom 1 pinch / 1g. (yes) - cool - sweet...................................earth
Salt 1 pinch / 1g. (yes) - cold - salty ........................................................water

**Cooking instructions:**
Wash and clean vegetables and divide into pieces. Puree all ingredients in a blender.

## 9.39 Sugar pea soup with prawns

Strengthens spleen and liver, regulates Qi flow, strengthens the middle, diuretic, harmonizes Qi (in the middle and lower heater), forces kidney-Qi und -Yang
Cooking time approx. 15 min
Calories p. portion: 215
3 portions
Allergens: BL

**Quantity of ingredients:**
Peas 5/8 lbs - 8oz / 250g. (yes) - neutral - sweet, salty..............................water
Basic recipe for a vegetable soup (nutritious) 2 cup / 500g. (yes) - neutral - *. *
Olive oil 1 teaspoon / 3g. (little) - cool - sweet............................................earth
Onion (spring onion) 1 piece / 20g. (yes) - warm - acrid ...........................metal
Parsley 1 Bunch / 15g. (yes) - warm - bitter .............................................. wood
Olive oil 1 teaspoon / 3g. (little) - cool - sweet............................................earth
Shrimp 8 pieces / 120g. (yes) - warm - salty .............................................water
Salt 1 pinch / 0,5g. (yes) - cold - salty .......................................................water
Pepper (ground) 1 pinch / 0,1g. () - warm - acrid ......................................metal

**Cooking instructions:**
Cook the peas in a saucepan with water until soft, strain and quench with cold water. Mince the parsley, add to the peas and pour in the vegetable broth. Chop onions and fry in a little olive oil, add to soup and puree. Sauté the prawns in olive oil, cut into bite-sized pieces and add to the soup. Season with salt and pepper.

## 9.40 Tae from Dandelionroots

Cools liver fire, reduces internal heat, softens knots.
Cooking time approx. 15 min
Calories p. portion: 1
2 portions

**Quantity of ingredients:**
Dandelion (young plants) 2-4 teaspoons / 6g. (rec.) - cool - sweet, bitter .....fire
Water 2 cup / 500g. (yes) - cool - salty......................................................earth

**Cooking instructions:**
The chopped dandelion is doused with cold water. Heat the whole thing until it boils and cook for a minute. Then let
it rest for ten minutes, filter and enjoy ... Sweet to taste with honey.

## 9.41 Tea from celery sticks

Brings the Liver Qi in motion, cools heat, moisturizes, relaxes, builds up Qi, spreads.
Cooking time approx. 15 min
Calories p. portion: 1
4 portions
Allergens: L

**Quantity of ingredients:**
Celery sticks 2 table spoons (chopped) / 18g. (rec.) - cool - sweet ............earth
Water 2 cup / 500g. (yes) - cool - salty......................................................earth

**Cooking instructions:**
Heat the water till it boils and put it aside. Add cutted celery and cook for 10 min. to let go. Strain. Sweet to taste with honey.

## 9.42 Tea from lavender blossoms

Cooking time approx. 10 min
Calories p. portion: 0
1 portion

**Quantity of ingredients:**
Lavender blossoms 1 teaspoon / 2g. () - warm - acrid, bitter .......................... *
Water 1 cup / 125g. (yes) - cool - salty......................................................earth

**Cooking instructions:**
Heat the water till it boils and put it aside. Add lavender flowers and 10 min. to let go. Sweet to taste with honey. Strain when pouring.

## 9.43 Tea from rosemary

Dries out, passes downwardly, forces heart, lung and spleen Qi, forces liver-blood, forces heart-Yin, expels spleen heat / cold moisture, strengthens spleen and kidney Yang.
Cooking time approx. 15 min
Calories p. portion: 1
4 portions

**Quantity of ingredients:**
Rosemary 2-4 teaspoons / 6g. (rec.) - warm - bitter......................................fire
Water 2 cup / 500g. (yes) - cool - salty......................................................earth

**Cooking instructions:**
Heat the water till it boils and put it aside. Add rosemary and 10 min. to let go. Strain. Sweet to taste with honey.

## 9.44 Tea from thyme

Converts mucus, forces lungs and spleen, dries out, passes downwardly.
Cooking time approx. 10 min
Calories p. portion: 0
4 portions

**Quantity of ingredients:**
Thyme 3 table spoons / 6g. (rec.) - warm - bitter.............................................. *
Water 2 cup water / 500g. (yes) - cool - salty .............................................earth

**Cooking instructions:**
Heat the water till it boils and put it aside. Add thyme and 10 min. to let go. Strain. Sweet to taste with honey.
Drink 2 to 3 cups daily by mouth

## 9.45 Tea Green tea

Reduces internal heat, dissolves mucus, detoxifies.
Cooking time approx. 10 min
Calories p. portion: 2
1 portion

### Quantity of ingredients:
Green tea 1 teaspoon / 2g. (rec.) - cool - sweet, bitter ...................................fire
Water 1 cup / 120g. (yes) - cool - salty......................................................earth

### Cooking instructions:
For each cup you use a teaspoonful or a teabag.
Pour green tea only with 60 to 80 ° C / 140 to 176 °F hot water, otherwise it will be bitter.
If the tea has a stimulating effect, let it draw for two to three minutes. It has a calming effect for a duration of five minutes (no longer, otherwise it will be bitter!).
Another method: Pour the tea leaves with about 70 ° C / 158 °F hot water and pour the water immediately again. Then just pour hot water again. The bitter substances disappear and the tea gets a milder aroma.

## 9.46 Tea mixture against general exhaustion

Cooking time approx. 10 min
Calories p. portion: 2
4 portions

### Quantity of ingredients:
Lemon Balm (dried) 2 teaspoons / 3g. (yes) - cool - sour..........................metal
Blackberry leaves 2 teaspoons / 3g. () - neutral - bitter...................................*
Lavender blossoms 1 teaspoon / 2g. () - warm - acrid, bitter ..........................*
Water 1 1/2 cups / 500g. (yes) - cool - salty...............................................earth

### Cooking instructions:
Heat the water till it boils and put it aside. Add 2 g lemon balm, 2 g blackberry leaves, 1,5g lavender flowers, leave to stand covered for 10 minutes, then strain. Drink a cup three times a day.

## 9.47 Thick pea soup

Nourishes Qi, diuretic, harmonizes Qi (especially in the Middle and Lower), strengthens the kidney and the defense Qi, dischars moisture.
Cooking time approx. 2-3 hours
Calories p. portion: 123
3 portions
Allergens: AN

**Quantity of ingredients:**
Peas, green 3/8 lbs - 6oz / 150g. (yes) - neutral - sweet ........................... water
Water 2 1/4 cups / 550g. (yes) - cool - salty ............................................... earth
Sesame oil 1 table spoon / 20g. (little) - cool - sweet ................................ earth
Onion white 1/2 piece / 25g. (yes) - warm - acrid ..................................... metal
Ginger fresh 1/2 teaspoon / 1g. (yes) - warm - acrid ............................... metal
Ground 1/2 teaspoon / 1g. (yes) - warm - acrid ........................................ metal
Oat meal 1 table spoon / 15g. (yes) - warm - sweet ................................. metal
Salt 1 pinch / 1g. (yes) - cold - salty ........................................................ water
Parsley 1 stem / 2g. (yes) - warm - bitter .................................................. wood

**Cooking instructions:**
Soak dried peas before cooking. Sauté sesame oil, onion, a little oatmeal, ginger and cumin in a hot pot; add the peas and simmer for 2-3 hours; add salt at the end and purée with a blender; garnish with parsley.

## 9.48 Tsampa

Reduces internal heat, dissolves mucus, detoxifies.
Cooking time approx. 5 min
Calories p. portion: 140
2 portions
Allergens: A

**Quantity of ingredients:**
Tsampa 4 table spoons / 30g. (yes) - cold - sweet, little salty .................... earth
Green tea 1 cup / 120g. (rec.) - cool - sweet, bitter ..................................... fire
Water 1 cup / 120g. (yes) - cool - salty ....................................................... earth

**Cooking instructions:**
Tsampa is traditionally made with tea.
The Tsampa is poured into a bowl and doused with tea, part of which is drunk and the remainder made into a dough-like mass with Tsampa. You can also pour the tea first; In any case, it takes some skill to achieve the right balance of Tsampa and liquid. The two substances are

usually mixed with your fingers. It is recommended to add yak butter to improve taste and stability.

## 9.49 Vegetable miso soup with tofu

Strengthens spleen and liver, regulates Qi flow, moisturizes, relaxes, builds up Qi, spreads, forces Qi, forces liver and kidney, reduces damp heat, detoxifies, nourishes fluids, reduces internal heat, dries out, passes downwardly.
Cooking time approx. 15 min
Calories p. portion: 107
4 portions
Allergens: EN

### Quantity of ingredients:
Sesame oil 2 table spoons / 35g. (little) - cool - sweet ...............................earth
Onion (shallot) 1 piece / 20g. (yes) - warm - acrid, sweet ........................ metal
Carrot 1 piece / 70g. (yes) - neutral - sweet ...............................................earth
Leek 2 inches / 10g. (yes) - warm - acrid ................................................. metal
Water 3 cups / 750g. (yes) - cool - salty.....................................................earth
Endive salad 2 table spoons / 30g. (yes) - neutral - bitter ...........................fire
Soy Tofu 2 table spoons / 30g. (rec.) - cool - sweet ...................................earth
Ginger fresh 1/2 teaspoon / 1g. (yes) - warm - acrid ................................. metal
Miso 2 table spoons / 15g. (yes) - neutral - salty.......................................water

### Cooking instructions:
In sesame oil first sauté onions, then carrots and a little leek; Pour in water and simmer gently; add the bean sprouts and endive leaves and leave to stand; Tofu cubes, add a little ginger; at the end stir in a little cooled cooking-water the Miso.

## 9.50 Vegetable potato and meat mash

Strengthens spleen and liver, regulates Qi flow, moisturizes, relaxes, builds up Qi.
Cooking time approx. 30 min
Calories p. portion: 127
2 portions

### Quantity of ingredients:
Potato 1/4 lbs - 4oz / 100g. (yes) - neutral - sweet......................................earth
Carrot (Early Carrot) 5/8 oz / 200g. (yes) - neutral - sweet.........................earth
Beef meat (calf) 1/8 lbs - 2oz / 40g. (yes) - neutral - sweet.......................earth
Apricots juice 6 table spoons / 60g. (little) - warm - sweet..........................earth
Rapeseed oil 1 table spoon / 6g. (little) - neutral - sweet............................earth

**Cooking instructions:**
Remove the flesh, skin, tendons and grease, wash under cool water and cut into small pieces and boil in a little water. After about 15-20 minutes, remove and puree. Wash the vegetables and potatoes, peel and cut into not too small pieces. Cook gently with a little water over a low heat for 10-20 minutes. Use the blender to chop the vegetables. Mix everything, add butter or oil and fruit juice and puree again.

Alternately use other meats such as chicken, lamb or turkey. Also change vegetables with zucchini, kohlrabi, fennel, pumpkin, parsnips and broccoli.

Also change the fruit juices. This can produce a variety of flavors.

## 9.51 Warming carrot soup

Forces Qi und warms Yang.
Cooking time approx. 30 min
Calories p. portion: 133
3 portions
Allergens: HL

**Quantity of ingredients:**
Carrot 4 pieces / 250g. (yes) - neutral - sweet ............................................earth
Walnut oil 2 table spoons / 20g. (little) - neutral - sweet..............................earth
Onion (shallot) 2 pieces / 40g. (yes) - warm - acrid, sweet........................ metal
Anise (Common Fennel) 1/2 teaspoon / 1g. (yes) - warm - acrid ...............earth
Nutmeg 1 pinch / 1g. (little) - warm - acrid.................................................. metal
Ginger fresh 1/2 teaspoon / 1g. (yes) - warm - acrid ................................. metal
Salt 1 pinch / 1g. (yes) - cold - salty .......................................................... water
Basic recipe for a vegetable soup (nutritious) 2 cup / 500g. (yes) - neutral - *. *
Parsley 1 table spoon / 10g. (yes) - warm - bitter...................................... wood

**Cooking instructions:**
Heat walnut oil in a hot pot and fry onions; steam the carrots in it; add anise, nutmeg, a little ginger, salt and sauté everything; add water or vegetable- or meat stock; cook everything soft and then puree; fold in parsley at the end.

Recommendation: Suitable for the cold season, especially if you use meat broth as a liquid for infusion.

# 10 Effects of food

## 10.1 Use ingredients: recommendable

Acai powder
Acerola fruit nectar or powder
Adzuki beans
Agave nectar
Agrimony
Aloe juice
Amaranth
Amaranth Pops
Angelica root
Apple puree
Apricot dried
Apricot jam
Apricot nectar
Apricots juice
Baking powder
Banchatee (green tea)
barberry
Barley
Barley flour
Barley grass powder
Barley grouts
Barley malt
Barley not peeled
Basic recipe for a beef soup
Basic recipe for a fish soup
Bay leaf
Bean oil
Beans (green, fresh)
Bearberry leaf
Beef bone marrow
Beef heart
Beef heart (calf)
Beef kidney
Beef lungs (calf)
Beef Oxtail pieces
Beef soup meat
Beer (alcohol-free)
Beer (alcohol-reduced)
Berries of the season
Berry juice
Bitter Herb liqueur
Bitter Lemon
Bitter liqueur
Black fungus mushroom
Blackberry dried (unripe fruit)
Blackberry jam
Blackberry leaves
Blackthorn (Sloe)
Blue mallow tee

Blueberry dried
Blueberry jam
Bocksdorn fruits (Fructus Lycii, Goji, goji berry dried
Brazil nuts
Bread roll
Bread with carob kernel flour
Breadcrumbs (wheat bread, bread roll)
Brie cheese
Buckbean
Buckwheat whole grain
Burdock root tea
Butter (half fat)
Camembert
Campari
Capers in olive oil
Carambola (Star fruit)
Cardamom
Carob flour, St. john's bread
Celery sticks
Chamomile
Chamomile tea
Channa-Dal
Cherry (sour)
Cherry compote
Chervil
Chervil dried
Chicken Blood
Chicken egg white
Chicken heart
Chicken meat
Chicken yolk
Chickweed
Chicory
Chinese pearl barley
Chocolate (Diabetic)
Chrysanthemum blossom tea
Clarified butter
Clementine
Coconut fat
Coconut meat
Codfish
Coix (seeds) YiYi Ren
Cola drink
Cola drink (low calorie)
Compote (fruits of the season)
Corn (fast polenta)
Corn (roasted)
Corn flour

Corn germ oil
Corn starch
Cottage cheese
Cranberries
Cranberry
Cranberry jam
Cream (30% fat)
Cream 10% coffee cream
Cream sour 10%
Cream sour 20%
Cream sour 30%
Creamer
Crispbread
Crucian
Cucumber
Cucumber (bitter)
Cucumber (spicy cucumber)
Currant jam (black)
Currant jam (red)
Currant juice (black)
Currants (black)
Currants (red)
Curry paste red
Daisy
Dandelion (young plants)
Dandelion juice
Dandelionroots tea
Dashi
Dates red
Deer meat
Deer's Bones
Deer's kidneys
Duck (heart)
Duck (slaughtered)
Ducks egg
Dyer's broom herb
Edam cheese
Eel smoked
Elderberries
Emmental cheese
Fennel seeds ground
Fennel tea
Fenugreek (Trigonella foenum-graecum)
Fernet Branca (herbal bitter liqueur)
Feta cheese
Fish innards
Fish remains
Fish sauce
Flounder
Flower pollen
Fox nut, gorgon nut, makhana
Fresh cheese from soya
Fresh cheese with herbs

Freshwater crab
Fructose (glucose)
Fruit mix juice
Fruit tea
Gail plum
Galangal
Garam Masala powder
Gelatin white
Gelee Royal
Gentian root
Gentian root tea
Ginkgo fruit
Ginseng
Ginseng liqueur
Ginseng root
Goat and sheep's blood
Goat and sheep's brain
Goat and sheep's liver
Goat and sheep's stomach
Goose blood
Goose fat
Gorgonzola
Gouda cheese
Grapeseed oil
Green tea
Greengage
Guava
Halibut (Flatfish)
Hawthorn
Herbal tea mix
Herbs bitter
Hibiscus
Hibiscus tea
Hijiki
Hokkaido pumpkin
Honey wine (Met)
Hop
Horehound leaves
Horse meat
Iceberg lettuce
Jasmine blossoms tee
Jellyfish
Kaki plum
Kalmus
King Solomon's-seal
Kudzu
Kukicha tea
Ladyfingers
Lamb kidneys
Lamb liver
Lamb's lettuce
Lavender blossoms
Lemon Balm (dried)
Lemon Balm (fresh)

Lemongrass
Licorice root tea
Lily bulbs
Lime blossom tea
Linseed
Linseed (crushed)
Liver smoothing tea
Loquate / Japanese medlar
Lotus roots
Lotus seeds
Lovage seeds
Luo Han Guo fruit
Lychee liqueur
Lye roll
Mackerel
Mango juice
Manioc flour
Mare's milk
Martini
Mascarpone cheese
Mayonnaise 50%
Mayonnaise 80%
Medlar
Mineral water
Miso black (fermented)
Mixed Pickles
Mu Erh Mushroom
Muesli
Mulled Wine Spice
Multi-grain bread (gray bread)
Mung bean
Mung bean sprouting
Mustard
Mustard Dijon
Mustard medium hot
Mustard sweet
Nasturtium (nose-twister or nose-tweaker)
Nectarine
Nettles
Noodles (wheat) with egg
Noodles (wheat, lasagne) with egg
Noodles (wheat, ribbon noodles) with egg
Noodles (wheat, spaghetti) with egg
Noodles (whole grain) with egg
Nori, purple seaweed, red algae
Nutmeg
Oat
Oat flakes (whole grain)
Oat flakes roasted
Oat flour
Oat fusion (baby food)
Oat meal

Octopus
Olives green
Orange blossom
Orange dried peel
Orange jam
Orange peel
Oregano fresh
Oyster shell powder
Palm oil
Passion blossoms tea
Passion fruit
Peanut (roasted)
Peanut butter
Pearl barley
Pearl barley
Pepper powder (hot)
Peppermint
Peppermint tea
Pepperoni
Pepperoni, yellow, pitted, halved
Peppers powder
Pig blood
Pigeon
Pigeon egg
Plum dried
Pork Bacon
Pork brain
Pork fat (lard)
Pork ham
Pork ham cooked
Pork ham smoked
Pork heart
Pork kidneys
Pork knuckle
Pork Lard
Pork liver
Pork lung
Pork marrow bones
Pork sausage (Bratwurst)
Pork skin
Pork stomach
Pork/beef sausage (smoked)
Pork's intestine
Potato (mealy)
Potato flour
Prickly pear
Processed cheese 12%
processed cheese 30%
Prosecco
Psyllium seed
Pudding powder vanilla
Puff pastry
Pumpernickel (dark bread)
Rabbit (wild)

Radicchio
Raspberry jam
Raspberry leaf tea
Red beet
Ribworttea
Rice (Gaoliang / Sorghum)
Rice mash
Rice round grain
Rice starch
Rice sticky
Rice wild (nature rice)
Rose blossom tea
Rose hip
Rose leaf tea
Rosefish
Rosemary
Rum
Rusk
Rye wholemeal bread
Safflower (Dyer's thistle  / Hong Hua)
Sago (cereals)
Salt
Salt (herbal)
Sea cucumber
Sesame oil roasted
Sesame paste (Tahini)
Sesame, black
Sesame, white
Sheep's milk yoghurt
Sherry (whine)
Shrimps
Skim milk powder
Slug
Soy flour
Soy noodles
Soy Tofu
Soy Tofu smoked
Soya Cuisine (soy cream)
Soybean milk
Soybeans
Soybeans, blacks, fermented
Spelled flakes
Spurdog (spiny dogfish, Schillerlocken)
St. Benedict's thistle, blessed thistle,
holy thistle, spotted thistle
Stevia (candyleaf, sweetleaf)
Strawberry jam
Sugar - icing sugar
Sugar brown
Sugar molasses
Sugar palm sugar
Sugar substitute (sweetener)
Supplementary nutrition
Tabasco

Tea mixture uric acid lowering
Thyme
Thyme dried
Toast bread (whole grain)
Tomato dried
Tomato juice
Tomato paste
Tomato puree
Tonic Water
Trout (smoked)
Truffle
Tsampa (roasted barley flour)
Turkey breast meat
Turkey ham
Turmeric (yellow root)
Turnip
Turnips
Umeboshi paste
Valerian
Vanilla pod
Vanilla sugar natural
Vinegar Aceto Balsamico white
Walnuts roasted
Watermelon
Wax gourd
Wheat beer
Wheat bran
Wheat flatbread/pita bread
Wheat flour whole grain
Wheat/Rye/Gray-black bread with yeast
Wheatgrass juice
Wheatgrass powder
Whey
White bread (baguette)
White bread (pretzel sticks)
White bread (roll)
White bread (wheat bread)
White breadcrumbs
White dumpling bread (wheat bread cut
into chunks)
Whitefish
Whole grain bread
Wholemeal flour
Wild garlic (garlic spinach)
Wild herbs
Wild strawberries
Wormwood
Wormwood herb
Yam root, yam root tuber
Yarrow
Yeast
Yew nut
Yoghurt vanilla

## 10.2 Use ingredients: yes

Agar agar (kelp)
Almond
Anise (Common Fennel)
Apple (sweet)
Apple juice (natural cloudy)
Apricots
Arrowroot
Artichoke
Asparagus (green or white)
Aubergine
Avocado
Basic recipe for a duck soup
Basic recipe for a vegetable soup
(nutritious)
Basil
Basil (fresh)
Batavia
Beef fillet
Beef liver
Beef meat
Beef meat (calf)
Beef meatbones
Beef stomach
Bitter orange peel
Black beans
Black caraway
Black-eyed peas
Boletus mushroom
Borage
Boxhorn clover seeds
Broad beans (thick beans)
Broccoli
Brussels sprouts
Buckwheat
Bush beans
Butter beans white
Calamari
Carp
Carrot
Carrot (Early Carrot)
Carrot juice without sugar
Cashews
Cauliflower
Caviar
Celery root
Champignon
Chanterelle
Chard
Chenpi (chinese tangerine bowl)
Chickpeas
Chinese cabbage

Chives
Chlorella (fresh water)
Clove

Coriander
Coriander (fresh)
Corn
Corn silk tea
Cress
Cumin (Caraway seed)
Curcuma
Curry
Deer meat
Dill
Elderberry blossom tee
Endive salad
Fennel
Fig
Fig dried
Fish pieces mixed (fresh water)
French beans
Freshwater fish
Ginger fresh
Goose
Goose parts
Gourd
Grapefruit (Pomelo)
Grapefruit dried peel
Grapefruit juice
Ground
Ground caraway
Hazelnuts
Herbs of Provence
Herbs various
Herbs wild
Hyssop
Juniper berry
Kidney beans (red)
Kohlrabi
Kombu seaweed (Saccharina japonica)
Leaf salads (bitter)
Leek
Lemon peel
Lentils
Lentils black
Lentils red
Lentils yellow
Lima beans
Lovage
Marjoram
Millet

Millet flakes
Miso
Miso paste (soy bean paste)
Morel (black, dried)
Morel, dried
Mussels
Mustard seeds
Octopus
Olives
Onion (shallot)
Onion (spring onion)
Onion read
Onion white
Orange grated peel
Oregano dried
Oysters
Parsley
Parsley root
Parsnip
Peas
Peas, green
Peppers (rose peppers)
Peppers (sweet)
Perch
Pheasant
Pinto beans speckled
Pistachios
Potato
Pumpkin seeds
Quail
Quail egg
Quince
Quinoa
Rabbit
Rabbit liver
Rabbit meat
Radish
Radish (white, green, purple-red)
Radish black
Radish horseradish
Radish leaves

Raisins
Red cabbage
Reishi mushroom
Rice (fragrance)
Rice (whole grain)
Rice Basmati
Rice black
Rice flour
Rice long grain rice
Rice variety any
Romaine lettuce / lettuce salad
Rye
Rye flour
Saffron
Sage
Salmon
Salsify
Savory
Savoy cabbage / kale
Seacrab
Shiitake, dried
Sour milk cheese 20%
Soy sauce
Soybeans, black
Soybeans, yellow
Spinach
Star anise
Sunflower seeds
Tarragon (Estragon)
Trout
Umeboshi plums (Japanese apricots)
Vanilla
Vanilla powder
Vegetable juice
Wakame
Water
Water hot
White beans
White cabbage
Yarrow tea
Zucchini

## 10.3 Use ingredients: little

Almond marzipan
Almond milk
Almond puree
Apricot
Borage oil
Cereal coffee
Cherry
Cherry juice
Chestnuts

Coconut flakes
Coconut grated
Coconut milk
Cooking oil
Corn Grease (Polenta)
Dates dried
Dulse (seaweed)
Evening primrose oil
Ginger oil

Goose egg
Grape juice red
Grape juice white
Grapes red
Grapes white
Grass carp
Linseed oil
Malt
Margarine
Margarine (diet)
Oat milk
Okra
Olive oil
Oyster mushroom
Peaches
Peaches (canned)
Peanut oil
Peanuts
Pear
Pear juice
Pepper white (ground)

Peppers
Pine nuts
Pork meat
Pumpkin
Pumpkin seed oil
Rapeseed oil
Rice malt
Rice noodles
Rice red
Rice sweet
Sesame oil
Soybean oil
Sunflower oil
Sweet potato
Thistle oil
Topinambur
Walnut oil
Walnuts
Wheat germ oil
Wild boar meat

## 10.4 Do not use contra-acting foods

Anchovy / Sardine
Apple (sour)
Balm
Bamboo shoots
Banana
Banana (cooking banana)
Basic recipe for a beef soup (warming)
Basic recipe for a chicken soup (warming)
Basic recipe for a rice soup (Congee)
Beer (Pils)
Beer (Top-fermented German dark beer)
Black tea
Blackberry´s
Blueberry
Blueberry juice
Brown ale
Buckwheat (roasted) Kasha
Bulgur (cereals)
Butter organic
Buttermilk
Cantaloupe
Chestnut puree
Chicken egg
Chicken liver
Chicken stomach
Chili (pod or ground)
Chocolate
Cinnamon ground

Cinnamon sticks
Clementines
Cocoa
Cod
Coffee
Couscous
Cow's milk (1.5% fat)
Cow's milk (whole milk 3.5% fat)
Crab
Cranberry
Cranberry juice
Cream, sweet 30%
Créme fraiche cheese
Curd cheese 20%
Curd cheese 40%
Currant (black)
Currant (red)
Currant (white)
Eel
Feta cheese
Fresh cheese
Garlic
Ginger powder
Goat
Goat and sheep's milk
Goat cheese
Gooseberry
Green spelt
Herring
Honey

Kefir
Kiwi
Kumquats
Lamb bones
Lamb meat
Lamb shoulder
Lamb's lettuce
Lemon
Lemon juice
Lettuce
Lime
Lobster
Longane
Lychee
Lychee in Preserved
Mallow (Malva sylvestris) blossom tea
Mango
Maple syrup
Mediterranean fish (cod, plaice, haddock, sea
Mirabelle plum
Mold cheese
Mozzarella
Mulberry fruit
Mullet
Mutton
Mutton
Orange
Orange juice
Papaya
Parmesan
Pepper (ground)
Pepper Cayenne
Peppercorns
Pepperoni, red, pitted, halved
Pickle
Pimento
Pineapple
Pineapple (from a can)
Pineapple juice without sugar
Plaice
Plum
Plums
Pomegranate
Poppy
Raspberry
Raspberry dried (immature)

Red berry (without sugar)
Red wine
Rhubarb
Rose hip tea
Rucola
Sake
Sauerkraut (cutted cabbage fermented)
Sea buckthorn
Shark
Sheep's milk
Shrimp
Sorrel
Sour cherries
Sour cream 15% fat
Sour milk
Sourdough
Spelled (Dark) bread
Spelled grain
Spelled semolina
Spelled wholemeal flour
Spiny lobsters
Spirit
Strawberries
Strawberry Juice
Sugar candy white
Sugar cane sugar
Sugar fructose - fruit sugar
Sugar glucose - grapes sugar
Sugar Milk Sugar
Sugar white
Tangerine
Tomato
Tuna
Vinegar (Apple vinegar)
Vinegar (Red wine vinegar)
Vinegar Aceto Balsamico
Wheat
Wheat bulgur
Wheat flakes
Wheat flour
Wheat semolina
Wheat semolina for children
White wine
Yogi tea
Yogurt (natural, 1.5% fat)
Yogurt (natural, 3.5% fat)

# 11  Complementary

## 11.1  Agrimony

Agrimonia eupatoria
Preparation: Healing tea (infusion)
Moves and regulates Liver-Qi and Gallbladder-Qi, astringent, quenches bleeding, strengthens Spleen-Qi and Stomach-Qi, transforms moisture, dissipates Moisture-Heat.
The herb contains many bitter and tannins and therefore helps as a tea in gastrointestinal diseases and liver disease. As a gargle, however, also relieves gingivitis, sore throat and coughing.
Dosage: 1-4 g of dried tea as a decoction, 1-4 ml tincture

## 11.2  Arctostaphylos uva-ursi (kinnikinnick)

Arctostaphylos uva-ursi (Ericaceae)
Preparation: Healing tea (infusion)
Clears damp heat in the lower heater, stops bleeding.
Side effects Nausea / Vomiting in stomach-sensitive persons due to the high tannin content. The cold macerate is easier on the stomach than the short decoction. Not during pregnancy, breastfeeding. Not for children under 12 years.
Dosage: Pour 2.5 g finely chopped or roughly powdered leaves over with 150 ml of boiling water and, after 15 minutes, pass
 through a tea strainer.

## 11.3  Bath with rosemary

Rosmarinus officinalis
Preparation: Healing bath
Tonifies middle of kidney yang, as well as kidney, heart, lung and spleen qi, gently moves liver qi, drains out wind-cold-
moisture stagnation, mildly stagnates blood, tones the heart. Blood.
Dosage: 1 Bag with 5g. rosemary. Put a tied bag with the rosemary in the water and let it soak for 10 minutes. The bag can be squeezed several times before removing it.
Note: Caution in pregnancy - has a stimulating effect on the uterus. Beware of Yin deficiency.

## 11.4 Birch leaves

Folium Betulae
Preparation: Healing tea (infusion)
Emits moisture, cools moisture-heat in the bladder. Heat cooling in bi-syndromes with wind, moisture.
Dosage: Pour 2 tablespoons of crushed birch leaves into 250 ml of boiling water, let stand for 10 minutes. Then sieve.
Drink one cup of it a day.

## 11.5 Burdock root

Radix Bardanae
Preparation: Healing tea (infusion)
Clarifying heat, eliminating toxins, dispelling wind-heat, eliminating heat, draining moisture across the bladder.
One of the best blood cleaners. Many toxins are excreted from the liver via the gallbladder, but some are excreted via the blood. The burdock root has the unique ability to release toxins through the bloodstream and helps to detoxify the liver.

Medical applications: abscesses, acne, anger, arthritis, blood cleansing, boils, bronchitis, lip ulcers, cancer, candida, chickenpox, colds, cough, bladder catarrh, dandruff, edema, eczema, gynecology, fever, flu, gout, hay fever, hives, hypoglycemia , Indigestion, inhibits tumors, irritability, jaundice, swollen joints, keratosis, kidney and liver problems, lymph congestion, measles, mumps, goat peter, obesity, pain, pneumonia, psoriasis, rheumatism, scabies, skin diseases, throat infections, sprains, staphylococci, urinary tract infections, uterine prolapse.

Properties: Alterative (gradually restores health), antibacterial, antibiotic, antifungal, anti-inflammatory, antipyretic, antitumoral, laxative, stimulates sex drive, choleretic, soothing, sweat-inducing, lactating, hypoglycemic, muco-stimulating, nourishing, rejuvenating.
Dosage: 10g / Liter

## 11.6 Corn silk

Zea mays, stigmata
Preparation: Healing tea (infusion)
Directs moisture-heat from the bladder, dissipates and clears the liver and gallbladder. Regulates bladder-Qi, diuretic.
Dosage: 10-30 g

## 11.7 Dandelion

Taraxaci
Preparation: Decoction
Reduces internal heat. Eliminates moisture-heat and heat-toxins.
Dischars moisture. Supports spleen-qi and stomach-qi.
Dosage: in case of liver and gall bladder problems and associated
tension, nausea and irritability, decoction with 6-8 plants for 10-14 days in
two doses on an empty stomach; with low milk production decoction from
10 plants in three doses on an empty stomach drink; for breast tumors
and associated pain and swelling decoction drink from 20 plants in three
doses on an empty stomach. Externally, the juice of the fresh plant acts
as an antidote to snake bites.
Special features: In TCM, the dandelion due to its decongestant,
decongestant and detoxifying effect as a remedy is of great
 importance in the treatment of disorders of the female reproductive
organs, especially the breasts, as well as liver complaints. In addition,
dandelion is very good to distribute the "hangover" the next morning after
copious consumption of alcohol.
Dosage: 6-8 plants in two doses on an empty stomach for 10-14 days
Note: Do not use too much as it is easy to get diarrhea.

## 11.8 Dead-nettles

Lamium album, herb.
Preparation: Healing tea (infusion)
Astringent in the lower heater, tonifies kidney-qi and spleen-qi, clears
damp- heat in the abdomen. Dissipating and cooling in bladder and
intestines. Cools Kidney-Yin and Heart-Yin.
Dosage: Pour 3 teaspoons of blossoms and cabbage with ¼ liter of
boiling water, infuse for 5 minutes and strain. Drink 3 cups of it daily.

## 11.9 Goldenrods leaves

Solidago virgaurea, herb.
Preparation: Healing tea (infusion)
Scatters moisture. Regulates Bladder-Qi, emits moisture-heat.

## 11.10    Juniper berries

Juniperus, fruct.
Preparation: Decoction
Dries out, heads down, activates Wei Qi. Relieves wind moisture and transforms. Tonifies Spleen-Qi, Stomach-Qi, Heart-Qi, Kidney-Qi and Kidney-Yang, warms the inside. Guides moisture and heat out of the bladder.
Use: tea, season
Dosage: Pour 2 teaspoons of the tea into 250 ml of boiling water and leave for 10 minutes. Then sieve. Drink 2 to 3 cups per day as needed.
Note: Avoid overdose, pregnant women and acute kidney patients should do without. External rubbing may cause blistering of the skin.


## 11.11    Silverweed roots

Argentina anserina
Preparation: Healing tea (infusion)
Regulates and moves qi-stagnation of the three warmers, astringent, quenches blood, clears heat, conducts moisture-heat.
Dosage: 5-10g dried leaves to 1 liter of water.


## 11.12    Sorrel

Rumex crispus, rad. / Rumex acetosa herb.
Preparation: Different effects
Eliminates moisture-heat, dissipates heat-toxins, regulates liver-qi and intestinal-qi, dissipates wind-cold and heat-wetness.
Dosage: Pour fresh or dried leaves with water and leave to soak for at least ten minutes.
Note: Do not use during pregnancy and lactation.


## 11.13    Willow bark

salix alba
Preparation: Healing tea (infusion)
Cools fire and heat. In bi-diseases: Wind, heat and moisture dissipating.
Dosage: 9-15 g

## 11.14  Wormwood

Artemisia absinthium, herb.
Preparation: Healing tea (infusion)
Strengthens Spleen-Qi and Stomach-Qi, moves Liver-Qi, regulates bile flow, dissipating Moisture-Heat and Heat, regulating the uterus.
Vermouth - Not only used to eliminate worms; it is also a highly effective liver and digestive aid. He also helps to remove blockages that produce a lethargic menstruation. It is always best to take this herbal remedy in conjunction with other herbs.

Medical applications: anemia, arthritis, bloating, circulatory system, colds, constipation, depression, edema, earache, fever, gynecology, wind, gallbladder, gallstones, gout, heartburn, hepatitis, jaundice, kidney disease, morning sickness, nausea, obesity, parasites, Rheumatism, stomach ailments, worms.

Properties: Abortive, alterative, appetite promoting, wormer, antibiotic, anti-depressant, anti-inflammatory, antipyretic, antiseptic, aromatic, bittertonikum, anti-flatulence, cholagogue, digestive, menstrual enhancer, stomach-strengthening, wormer.
Dosage: 1 tsp. To 1 / 2l water
Note: Do not use in pregnancy. It is always best to take this herbal remedy in conjunction with other herbs.

# 12 Basics of Nutrition

The basic principles of nutrition described herein are general recommendations. They are not aimed at a specific form of therapy. Recommendations concerning a therapy have priority.

## 12.1 Nutrition

Regular meals in a relaxed atmosphere. A warm breakfast is considered a good start into the day.
The main meals ought to be taken for lunch – supper in the early evening. Pay attention to feeling hungry or sated: don't eat too much nor remain hungry is the rule
Prepare the meals freshly from natural, regional products. Frozen, heat-conserved, industrially prepared or foodstuffs cooked in the microwave oven are rejected.
Choice of foodstuffs according to the season: more cooling food in summer, more warming food in winter.
Eat cooked food at least twice a day. Food and drinks ought to be lukewarm, never ice-cold or hot.
Raw vegetables, briefly cooked vegetables, freshly squeezed juices and mineral water are not recommended. Milk and dairy products are only included in the diet if they don't cause problems. Don't use therapeutic recipes over a longer period without consulting your doctor or therapist.

**Varied food**
Enjoy the diversity of foodstuffs. Characteristics of a balanced nutrition are variety, suitable combination and a balanced quantity of rich and low energy foodstuffs (on one hand avoiding undersupply with essential nutrients and on the other hand to take to many undesirable substances).

**A lot of Cereal Products - and Potatoes**
Bread, pasta, rice, cereal flakes (best wholemeal) as well as potatoes contain almost no fat, but many vitamins, mineral nutrients, trace elements, roughage and secondary plant substances. These foodstuffs ought to be taken with low-fat side dishes.

**Vegetables and Fruit – „Take Five" every day …** 5 portions of vegetables and fruit a day, as fresh as possible, briefly cooked, or maybe one portion as a juice – ideal as a side dish to every meal as well as snack between meals: Thus a lot of vitamins, mineral nutrients as well as roughage and secondary plant substances

**Daily milk and dairy products**

Milk and Dairy Products every Day, once or twice per Week Fish; meat, sausages as well as eggs moderately. These foodstuffs contain valuable nutrients like calcium in the milk, iodine selenium and omega-3 fat acids in saltwater fish. Meat is favorable due to its high content of disposable iron and the vitamins B1, B6 and B12. Quantities of 300 – 600 g meat and sausage per week are sufficient. Prefer low-fat products, especially in meat- and dairy products.

## Low-fat and fatty Foodstuffs
Fat supplies us with essential fat acids and fatty foodstuffs contain also fat-soluble vitamins. Fat is high in energy; therefore much fat in the food may cause overweight, possibly also cancer. Too many saturated fat acids may further a tendency for cardio-vascular diseases in the long term. Prefer vegetable oils and fats (e.g. rapeseed-, olive-, soya-oils and solid fats produced therefrom). Beware of invisible fat in meat- and dairy products, pastry and sweets as well as in fast-food and convenience foods. 70 – 90 g fat per day is sufficient.

## Moderately Sugar and Salt
Take sugar and foods/drinks containing various kinds of sugar (e.g. glucose syrup) only occasionally. Use herbs and spices as well as a little salt creatively. Prefer salt containing iodine.

## Plenty of Liquids
Water is absolutely essential. Drink 1-2 l liquids every day. Prefer water (with or without gas) and other low-calorie drinks. Alcoholic drinks should not be taken.

## Tasty Dishes, carefully cooked
Cook the meals with as low temperatures and as short as possible, using little water and fat – this preserves the original taste, keeps the nutrients intact and prevents the production of harmful compounds.

## Take time and enjoy the food
Take your Time and enjoy your Food
Eating consciously helps to eat right. The eye enjoys food, too. It's fun, invites to enjoy varied dishes and stimulates the feeling of satiety.

## Watch your Weight and stay in Motion
A balanced diet and a lot of exercise and sport (30 – 60 min/day) are a healthy combination. The right weight furthers well-being and health. Thermals, directional effectiveness, digestive power
There are various criteria for judging the effectiveness of herbs and

foodstuffs.

The use of certain herbs and ingredients is based on observations of the effects on the body which these foodstuffs, herbs and spices show after having eaten them. The medical science has developed following system: Every ingredient or herb has a directional effectiveness. Furthermore, there are herbs which have a special effect on certain organs.

The basic condition for a healthy metabolism is to obtain sufficient energy from food and that the digestive process doesn't use too much energy.

An easily digestible meal makes content and sated, doesn't cause flatulence and fatigue after the meal. The perfect spices increase the healthiness of our meals. Very often, just small doses of herbs and spices will suffice. They are not used to make us sated, but to help our digestive organs to digest the food.

## 12.2  Recipes

The recipes list the ingredients to be used and the cooking instructions show how the dish is prepared. The list of ingredients shows the concerned quantities as well as the relevance for the therapy. If you find „less than mentioned", try to comply or find an alternative from the „list of recommended foodstuffs". Mostly it shall result just in a small change of taste when you simply avoid this ingredient.

Mild cooking methods: boiling, stewing, poaching, steaming
Strong cooking methods: barbecuing, roasting, frying, smoking
Balanced cooking methods: deep-frying, baking brick
Deep-freezing and warming in the microwave oven should be avoided (denaturalization).

## 12.3  Foodstuffs

Foodstuffs have an effect on body and soul like medicinal herbs, only a very much milder one. Dietary advice is mainly based on regional foodstuffs. The knowledge about the effects of each foodstuff and the knowledge, when which foodstuff shall be used, is based on the orthodox school of medicine. Use ecologic-organic products, if possible. As everything should be cooked for a long time due to a better digestability and very rarely eaten raw, the food agrees with everyone.

The classification of the foodstuffs according to their effect on the body is the basis in order to achieve a harmonious status of health.

Dietary advisors do not recommend certain foodstuffs for everyone. The individual diet is tailor-made for the individual constitution.

Buy only fresh and ripe fruit and vegetables. You ought to leave unripe fruit and vegetables and such with brown spots and wilted leaves behind in the market. In this case take deep-frozen goods (never ready-to-serve dishes!). Fruit and vegetables are deep-frozen immediately after harvesting and often contain more vitamins and minerals than the goods from the vegetable shelf. Whereas conserved or tinned goods contain very much less biological substances. Also, salt, sugar and others are mostly added to the latter. Never leave the foodstuffs in the water after washing them to avoid that many vital substances get drowned. Clean salads, fruit and vegetables immediately before serving.

Please make sure of the hygienic processing of foodstuffs. Clean your salads, fruit and vegetables carefully. When cooking with meat, prepare all ingredients first and then process the meat products. Clean the worktop and tools very carefully. Wooden surfaces ought to be treated with a mild disinfectant regularly in order to reduce germination.
Store fruit and vegetables separately, if possible. Harvested fruit and vegetables are still alive and emit e.g. ethylene gas, which makes other products ripen and age faster. Keep meat and fish in the closed packaging or store them in the fridge in closed containers.

## 12.4 Herbs

There are some basic rules for storing medicinal herbs. On principle, herbs must be protected from direct sunlight, humidity and heat.

Containers for the storage of herbs may be glasses, ceramic jars and even plastic containers. However, plastic is a rather unsuitable material and should only be a short-term solution. In case of glass containers, use a dark material.

Medicinal herbs cannot be kept for any long period. The shelf life of herbs is limited. However, it can be prolonged with suitable storage. The place should be dark, rather cool and absolutely dry. A wooden medicine cabinet, placed not directly next to a source of heat, would be ideal. Never buy large quantities of herbs so as not to have to throw them away. Label the container with the name of the herb and the date of harvesting or processing.

# 13 Other dietic-books

The following syndromes of dietetics, TCM or for a therapy supplement for cancer are available.

## Dietetics

E001. Nutrition of the infant - baby food
E002. Nutrition during lactation
E003. Nutrition in old age
E004. Nutrition of children and adolescents
E005. Nutrition of athletes
E006. Light weight
E007. Pregnancy
E008. Full food

**Protein and electrolyte - kidneys**
E009. (hemodialysis) dialysis treatment
E010. Acute renal failure
E011. Chronic renal insufficiency
E012. Nephrotic syndrome
E013. Kidney stones (nephrolithiasis)

**Gastrointestinal tract - pancreas**
E014. Acute pancreatitis (inflammation of the pancreas)
E015. Chronic pancreatitis (inflammation of the pancreas)

**Gastrointestinal tract - small intestine and large intestine**
E016. Acute obstipation (constipation)
E017. Chronic obstipation (constipation)
E018. Colon irritabile
E019. Diverticulitis
E020. Acquired lactose intolerance (lactose malabsorption)
E021. Fructose malabsorption
E022. Glutensensitive enteropathy (celiac disease)
E023. Colectomy
E024. Short Bowel Syndrome

**Gastrointestinal tract - liver, gallbladder, bile ducts**
E025. Acute and chronic hepatitis (inflammation of the liver)
E026. Cholelithiasis (bile stones)
E027. fatty liver
E028. cirrhosis

**Gastrointestinal tract - Stomach and duodenal intestine**
E029. Acute gastritis
E030. Chronic gastritis
E031. Stomach bleeding
E032. Ulcus ventriculi and duodenal ulcer
E033. Condition after gastric surgery

### Gastrointestinal tract - oral cavity and esophagus
E034. Stomatitis
E035. Esophageal carcinoma (esophageal cancer)
E036. Refluosophagitis (heartburn)

### Special diseases
E037. Phenylketonuria (PKU)
E038. Rheumatic joint diseases

### Metabolism
E039. Obesity (overweight)
E040. Diabetes mellitus
E041. Eating disorders (underweight)

### Fat metabolism
E042. Hypercholesterolaemia (increased cholesterol level)
E043. Hepatic Encephalopathy

### Heart and circulation
E044. Arteriosclerosis (arterial calcification)
E045. Heart insufficiency
E046. Hypertension
E047. Hyperuricaemia and gout

### Changed nutrient requirements
E048. In case of fever
E049. For malignant diseases
E050. After burns
E051. Radiation and chemotherapy

## CANCER
E100. Pancreatic cancer
E101. Bladder cancer
E102. Blood cancer (leukemia)
E103. Breast cancer
E104. Colorectal cancer
E105. Gastric cancer
E106. Kidney cancer
E107. Esophageal cancer

## TCM
E200. Bladder - moisture heat in the bladder
E201. Bladder - moisture and cold in the bladder
E202. Bladder - emptiness and cold in the bladder
E203. Large intestine - external cold affects the large intestine
E204. Large intestine - moisture heat in the large intestine
E205. Large intestine - heat blocks the intestine II acute
E206. Large intestine - dryness of the colon
E207. Large intestine - Yang deficiency (cold)
E208. Heart - Blood insufficiency
E209. Heart - Blood stagnation
E210. Heart - Fire
E211. Heart - Hot mucus clogs the heart pores

E212. Heart - Cold mucus clogs the heart pores
E213. Heart - Qi deficiency
E214. Heart - Yang deficiency
E215. Heart - Yin deficiency
E216. Liver - Ascending Liver Yang
E217. Liver - Blood deficiency
E218. Liver - Blood stagnation
E219. Liver - Moisture heat in liver and gall bladder
E220. Liver - Fire
E221. Liver - Gall bladder Qi-Empty
E222. Liver - Cold in the liver meridian
E223. Liver - Qi stagnation
E224. Liver - Wind
E225. Liver - Wind with ascending liver Yang
E226. Liver - Wind with blood anemic
E227. Liver - Wind with extreme heat
E228. Lung - Qi deficiency
E229. Lung - Mucus-moisture in the lungs
E230. Lung - Mucus-heat in the lungs
E231. Lung - Mucus-cold in the lungs
E232. Lung - Dryness of the lungs
E233. Lung - Wind-heat attacks the lungs
E234. Lung - Wind-cold affects the lungs
E235. Lung - Yin deficiency
E236. Stomach - Bloodstagnation
E237. Stomach - Fire
E238. Stomach - Cold with liquid
E239. Stomach - Nutrition stagnation
E240. Stomach - Qi deficiency
E241. Stomach - Rebellious Qi
E242. Stomach - Yin Emptiness
E243. Spleen - Heat and moisture attack the spleen
E244. Spleen - Coldness and moisture affects the spleen
E245. Spleen - Qi deficiency
E246. Spleen - Qi deficiency + Declining spleen Qi
E247. Spleen - Qi deficiency + spleen does not control the blood
E248. Spleen - Yang deficiency
E249. Kidney - Heart and kidney no longer communicate
E250. Kidney - Jing deficiency
E251. Kidney - Kidneys cannot receive the Qi
E252. Kidney - Qi is not stable
E253. Kidney - Yang deficiency
E254. Kidney - Yin deficiency


For further information visit di-book.com.


# 14 EBNS - Software for nutritional counseling

The main task of the database is to create personalized nutritional advice for each patient individually. The database was developed for Dietetics

and Traditional Chinese Medicine.
The Database supports training and advices in the daily work routine.

The computer program provides lists of recipes, ingredients and herbs, which are given to the client. individually adjustable according to patient's request from whole food to vegetarians (lacto, ovo, ...). For every register there is an information sheet which can be given to the client. All texts can be individually designed.

The syndromes can be combined and result in an intersection of the recommended recipes and ingredients. The automated diagnosis for the TCM enables you to check your experience during the training as well as to confirm your diagnosis in the working day. You select several predefined symptoms and have the program automatically display the relevant syndromes.

How to work with the database:
Select the patient / client, select one or more of the syndromes you diagnosed and print the folder.

You can change all values, create new symptoms or syndromes, develop recipes, change or adapt ingredients and herbs to your findings. In simple client management, all relevant data about the person is stored. You get an overview of the past diagnoses and the development of the course of the disease.

As a consultant you save a lot of time when you print out the recipe, food and herbal lists for the recognized syndromes and give them to the clients. You can use this time for a personal conversation. With the database, dieticians and nutritionists can view the nutrients and trace elements for each recipe and develop recipes for syndromes even with suggested ingredients.

All recipe and grocery lists can also be ordered from me as a combination of several diseases. I wish all readers good luck, health and happiness in life.
More information can be found at www.ebns.at.
Volunteer: www.krebsinfo.at
Josef Miligui